ICO Investing

Understand the Initial Coin Offering and Cryptocurrency Investing

by

C.H. Robson

Table of Contents

Legal Notes	5
Introduction	6
Section 1: The Basics of Blockchain and Cryptocurrencies	8
Chapter 1. The Technology Behind Cryptocurrencies	9
In Blockchain we Trust	9
What is Blockchain?	10
The Importance of Blockchain	11
A Private Cryptographic Key	13
Bitcoin and Blockchain	14
The Increasing Difficulty of Bitcoin Mining	15
The Bitcoin Mining Process	16
Alternative Mining Methods	17
Chapter 2. Understanding Cryptocurrencies	18
How Does Cryptocurrency Work?	19
Categorization of Cryptocurrencies	20
Altcoins	20
Tokens	21
Types of Assets & Currencies	22
Chapter 3. Valuing Cryptocurrencies	25
The Difficulty in Assessing the Value of a Cryptocurrency	26
Factors Affecting the Value of a Cryptocurrency	27
Section 2: Investing - ICOs and Trading	30
Chapter 4. How ICOs Work	31
What is an ICO?	31
ICOs vs. IPO - What is the Difference?	32

Why Do Companies Choose ICO?	34
ICO Stages	34
Types of ICO Tokens	37
Chapter 5. Doing your Due Diligence	**38**
Technical and Fundamental Analysis for Cryptocurrencies	38
Importance of Due Diligence	39
How to Evaluate an ICO	39
Chapter 6. ICO Red Flags	**44**
Signs of Fraud	44
Red Flag 1: Unrealistic Offers	45
Red Flag 2: "Cryptocurrencies" Lacking the 3 Basic Criteria	47
Red Flag 3: Use Case Does Not Require Blockchain	48
Red Flag 4: Key Information is Not Available	48
Red Flag 5: No Public Discussion	49
Chapter 7: Trading Cryptocurrencies	**51**
Exchanges	51
Cryptocurrency Wallets	52
Types of Wallets	54
Picking a Cryptocurrency	57
Chapter 8. ICO Investing Strategy	**59**
Things to Keep In Mind When Investing	60
Strategy 1: Diversify Investments	61
Strategy 2: Invest for Bonus Offerings	62
Strategy 3: Invest in Low Token Caps ICOs	62
Strategy 4: Quick Flip Your Cryptocurrencies	62
Strategy 5: Hold the Tokens	63
Section 3: Looking to the Future	**64**
Chapter 9. The Future of ICOs	**65**

Trend 1: Increase in Scams 65
Trend 2: Regulation Will Continue to Increase 66
Trend 3: Regulation will result in Securities Tokens 67
Trend 4: VCs and Blockchain Will Fuel Each Other's Growth 68
Trend 5: Platforms Will Further Develop 68
Trend 6: Hard Forks Will Happen as Ideals Clash 69

Chapter 10: Regulating Cryptocurrencies 70

Self Regulation 70
Where Cryptocurrenices are Banned 71
Other Regulations Around the World 71

Conclusion 76

Legal Notes

Copyright 2018 - All rights reserved

This document contains opinions and ideas of the author. It is sold for the purpose of providing helpful and reliable information; the publisher, author, and all other parties involved in the making of this document are not required to render any qualified services or advice.

The information provided herein is strictly for educational purposes; any liability, in terms of inattention or otherwise, by any usage or abuse of any policies, processes, or directions contained within, is the solitary and utter responsibility of the reader.

Under no circumstances will any legal responsibility or blame be held against the publisher, author, or any other parties involved in the making of this document for any reparation, damages, or monetary loss due to the information herein, either directly or indirectly.

Permission is not granted to reproduce, duplicate, or transmit any part of this document in electronic or printed format. Recording of this publication is also prohibited and storage of this document is not allowed without the written permission from the publisher. All rights are reserved.

Introduction

In December of 2017 Bitcoin lost almost 22% in value over a course of four days. In January 2018 that downward trend continued until it hit a low of almost $7,000 in February. That is almost a 60% drop. This drop did not just affect Bitcoin; all major cryptocurrencies and Altcoins took a plunge in value as well with over $500 billion being wiped off the market capitalization.

Amid all the speculation, uncertainty, and panic you would expect that cryptocurrency would lose its appeal. However, what is happening is exactly the opposite. In fact, a survey by SurveyMonkey and the Global Blockchain Business Council found that almost 60% of Americans are aware of cryptocurrencies and additionally 70% of those surveyed are also optimistic that the value of cryptocurrencies will continue to rise in the next 5 years.

Initial Coin Offerings (ICOs) raised more capital in the first three months of 2018 alone than all of 2017. There are new cryptocurrencies being launched, and trading is becoming more popular than ever with 20% of financial firms looking to get in on trading in 2018. The popular cryptocurrency forums have at least doubled in size in the first three months of 2018 alone.

This increased popularity has resulted in more information, more conflicting viewpoints, and more hype. With it there are also more attempts at regulation as cryptocurrencies move from being the domain of tech geeks into the public limelight. With the increased interest in investing in Cryptocurrencies and ICOs, it pays to be well informed.

This book is structured into 3 sections.

Firstly, we will explore the basics of Blockchain and cryptocurrencies to ensure that you have a strong understanding of the technology and terms used in the cryptocurrency world. This is an important starting point as it will help you evaluate the feasibility of coins and tokens without getting intimidated by the technical terms being thrown about so commonly in the cryptocurrency blogs, news, and whitepapers. Also, by understanding what Blockchain can and cannot do, and how cryptocurrencies operate, hopefully, you will not fall victim to scams.

Secondly, we will explore investing and trading with a focus on ICOs as that is where I believe most of the opportunities lie and it is what you should be paying attention to. When investing in ICOs, you are betting on the future success of a project. Since there is no track record to consider before investing, you will have to base your decision to invest or not on the attributes that we look at in this section.

Thirdly, we will look at the expected future of cryptocurrencies in 2018 and beyond as this will certainly shape your choices and investments in time to come. The chapters in these sections are intended to bring you up to speed with the recent developments in the cryptocurrency world and ease you into your future research.

A note before we go into the chapters: I make no claims on what you should or should not invest in, nor how you should invest in cryptocurrencies. The goal of this book is to help you to understand the factors you should be considering when choosing an ICO to back, or a cryptocurrency to invest in, as well as the strategies that you can use.

Always do your due diligence, keep up to date with the developments in the market, and never ever trust a get rich quick scheme!

Section 1: The Basics of Blockchain and Cryptocurrencies

Chapter 1. The Technology Behind Cryptocurrencies

To understand cryptocurrency, a logical place to start would be to understand the technology behind it. This would be Blockchain; an open, global, peer-to-peer platform that alters the fundamentals of what can be done online, as well as the manner in which we do it.

Blockchain itself brings a robust and different next-generation method to register and exchange tangible and intangible assets. As some experts have summarized it, the Blockchain is a digital medium for the exchange of value.

In Blockchain we Trust

Blockchain a technology that facilitates peer to peer transactions, this means that it removes the need for intermediaries by connecting parties directly. An example of this in the financial sector is the direct transfer of funds between parties without involving banks and financial institutions. However, it does this in a manner that keeps the identities of both parties confidential, by validating the information against prior transactions and keeping a record of all the transactions.

This means that any personal information acquired is private and not transmitted to the other party. It is possible for the buyer and seller to conduct a trade and pay for goods and services without either party knowing the identity of the other. This is because the transaction is reconciled through mass collaboration and then encrypted and stored in a digital ledger.

The Blockchain system has the ability to hold documents ranging from title deeds, educational degree certificates, to legal contracts, or even personal identification. This is due to the fact that Blockchain permits smart contracts. This is a computer protocol intended to facilitate, verify, and enforce a contract digitally in a verifiable and irreversible manner.

This makes it a ledger or record of transactions, shared across multiple computers. Because Blockchain can be used in the context of many different types of operations, we need to identify a list of characteristics that define and differentiate Blockchain ledgers from the rest.

Blockchain transactions:

- Are recorded on multiple nodes
- Takes place on a peer-to-peer (P2P) network
- Are created and accessed by peers
- Are encrypted
- Uses a digital signature to verify identities

The above list of features is what differentiates a Blockchain from a regular database. Most notably, new entries are distributed to other nodes in the network which updates the database universally. These updates are done through the network and comply with the agreed upon requirements.

What is Blockchain?

Blockchain was originally designed as an accounting framework for the cryptocurrency known as Bitcoin, which was supposed to address unified, controlled monetary standards that were subject to fluctuations in value. It was intended to be a digital currency that would avoid the fluctuations caused by real world market factors. The first Blockchain was therefore implemented by Bitcoin.

So how then does the Blockchain work? Using Bitcoin as an example, when we buy a product using cryptocurrency the Blockchain network creates a transaction. The funds are then transferred from a digital wallet, and confirmed by all the nodes (users) running the Blockchain. This is checked against the ledger in the Blockchain to ensure that there is sufficient funds to perform the transaction, and then it is added to the Blockchain as another transaction.

These transactions are recorded on the Blockchain using a hash function. This breaks down the transaction into a series of characters, which is performed by the software, creating a complex mathematical problem. This is then solved using sheer computing power, which may take trillions of attempts, and then verified by other peers. This solving of mathematical problems is known in the cryptocurrency world as "mining", as those that solve these problems are rewarded with an amount of cryptocurrency. The hashes that are solved are entered into the ledger of the Blockchain and are then confirmed.

This makes each transaction both secure and transparent as it can be seen by all nodes or users, preventing any possibility of fraud. This also keeps records private and safe, as the transactions are stored as encrypted blocks on the Blockchain.

The Importance of Blockchain

The Blockchain is essentially a decentralized online platform that deals with contracts. In terms of cryptocurrency, this refers to financial transactions, but it can be used for other contracts such as identity data, product or component history, or any type of data. What is important is the decentralization of the platform, which means that the data exists in more than one location.

The current online payment gateways such as PayPal and other eWallets are integrated with a bank account or credit card to send and receive money. Blockchain being decentralized exists as code across a network, which bypasses these middlemen such as PayPal, eWallets, or banks.

The main traits of the Blockchain are:

1. It keeps a record of all transactions.
2. It is able to establish contracts.
3. It is able to establish identities.

These three services explained above are usually performed by financial institutions and middle men, and the decentralization of these roles means that these middle men can be replaced by the Blockchain. With the huge market capital of the financial industry, replacing these roles with the Blockchain would have a great impact of disrupting the industry. It might even result in increased efficiency within the business if implemented correctly.

Outside the financial industry, the ability to establish contracts plays an important role as it keeps a record of an activity between two parties. Blockchain is able to store information digitally as encrypted codes. By entering a unique key, individuals are able to "sign in" and agree to or execute a contract.

Using this system, it is possible for "smart technology" to be used to connect objects with companies. Monitoring software could be used to control the access to items or locations, which can be useful in issuing electronic tickets to events or movies. The same technology could be used to keep records with certain devices and transmit them to authorities, such as in the use of equipment; these records can then be used for billing purposes or to monitor the condition of equipment for servicing. Because of the fraud proof capability of Blockchain, it is able to be put to use in many different aspects in a myriad of industries.

A Private Cryptographic Key

A private cryptographic key is a variable that is used with an algorithm to encrypt and decrypt codes. While the algorithm itself does not need to be kept secret, the key should be. This gives privacy and security to the person holding the key, and this is not even shared with the other party in the transaction.

Each Blockchain transaction generates a signature from the private key, and without the key it is impossible to make a fraudulent transaction. It is therefore very important to keep your private key secure, and not to share it with anyone.

Bitcoin and Blockchain

To further understand Blockchain, it is important to understand Bitcoin. Bitcoin is an electronic currency, started in late 2008. It was originally intended as a peer-to-peer electronic virtual currency system, allowing individuals to buy, sell, trade, and hold them as assets. As each transaction does not require a bank or financial institution to authenticate, any Bitcoin transaction is intended to be almost instantaneous, and are secured after an hour from submission.

The main use of Bitcoin is for peer-to-peer transactions, serving as a medium of exchange similar to any other currency like US Dollars, British Pounds, Euros, or Japanese Yen. You can exchange these currencies for good or services, like a meal at a restaurant, or clothes at a shop. Similarly, Bitcoin can serve the same purpose.

As with any brick-and-mortar cash transaction, there is no record of which individual gave which dollar bill. Although a transaction is known to have taken place, it does not pass through a bank or financial institution since there is an establishment of trust in the business, and in the currency. The proof of work in the currency of Bitcoin allows trust to carry out the transaction, and a third party financial institution is not needed.

The value of Bitcoin comes from the trust that exists between peers that participate in the market as it is not regulated by banks or governments; proof of work in the above example is sacrosanct to the value of the currency, as it ensures that the buyer has sufficient funds for the transaction, and the seller is receiving the correct amount for the sale. In this way, it is a currency or cash asset.

As proof of this, a number of businesses are already accepting Bitcoin as of the writing of this book. One example is Expedia, which has allowed users to pay for hotel bookings since June 2014. Microsoft also allows Bitcoins to be used, depositing them into your Microsoft account allows you to buy games, movies and other apps in the Windows and Xbox stores. Additionally, a number of businesses are accepting Bitcoins in their stores worldwide.

The Increasing Difficulty of Bitcoin Mining

There are only 21 million Bitcoins available, and as more and more Bitcoins are circulated, the longer it takes to mine one. Because of this, the more Bitcoins there are in the market, the harder it is to mine Bitcoins. It is estimated that it takes ten minutes on average to solve a block containing the latest transaction data by miners, with the help of cryptographic hash functions

Bitcoins are rewarded to miners when they validate transactions, and the network compensates them with digital coins for contributing with the necessary computational power to provide a proof of work. Naturally, the reward is directly proportional to the computing power a person contributes to solving the hashes. The more processing power you put in, the more coins you get for solving hashes.

This requires special programs and high-end computers, usually costing in the thousands of dollars in order to get the most efficiency. However, with the difficulty of hashing rapidly increasing, competition is high and as a result, the rewards are being claimed by the miners that are able to scale and solve the complex mathematical problems quickly and cheaply.

Also, the Bitcoin network is designed to produce a constant amount of Bitcoins every 10 minutes. With an increase in miners, the mathematical algorithms that are generated has to increase in order to adjust to the increase in the hash rate of the network. This artificially throttles the production of Bitcoins, making it harder to actually mine Bitcoins profitably.

The Bitcoin Mining Process

This is the mining process for Bitcoins:

Step 1: Every ten minutes pending Bitcoin transactions (a "block") is collected by miners and turned into a mathematical puzzle via algorithms.

Step 2: The miners try to solve the puzzle by guessing at random. Due to the hash function, it is impossible to predict the outcome as changing a single number or character will result in a vastly different hash. Therefore using a brute force technique and applying the hash function will eventually lead to the solution.

Step 3: The first miner to find the solution announces it to others on the network. The rest of the miners immediately switch over to validating the solution and the transaction. They check the answer to the mathematical puzzle, as well as ensure that the sender has sufficient funds to send over for the transaction.

Step 4: If there is a consensus that the solution is correct, the block is cryptographically added to the ledger and the miners move on to the next block of transactions.

Alternative Mining Methods

When looking at ICOs, it is important to understand how the cryptocurrency will be mined. Individual mining or "proof of work" is the standard model in the Bitcoin Blockchain, but as the difficulty of mining rises there have been innovative ways to optimize computing power and share the costs as well as the profits from mining, thus resulting in Cloud Mining and Mining Pools rising in popularity in late 2017.

Cloud Mining

As mining becomes more and more resource intensive, cloud mining has appeared recently to allow miners to mine cryptocurrency without managing the hardware. Instead, miners purchase "mining contracts", which enables them to buy the output of Bitcoins mined from the hardware during the term of their contract.

For example, if a miner were to purchase a mining contract for a day then whatever amount of Bitcoins mined from the cloud mining service in that day would belong to the miner.

Mining Pools

Mining pools are another way that miners are getting around the escalation of computing power required to mine cryptocurrencies like Bitcoin. This is done by combining the computing power of several miners; this method has gained in popularity as the difficulty of mining has increased to the point where it would take a huge amount of time to generate blocks. The rewards for mining pools are usually distributed according to the amount of computing power contributed.

Chapter 2. Understanding Cryptocurrencies

Now that you have an understanding of Blockchain technology, let us move on to the main topic: Cryptocurrencies.

Cryptocurrencies are digital or virtual currencies that are encrypted (secured) using cryptography. Cryptography refers to the use of encryption techniques to secure and verify the transfer of transactions. Bitcoin represents the first decentralized cryptocurrency, which is powered by a public ledger that records and validates all transactions chronologically, called the Blockchain.

The creation of Bitcoin precipitated the expansion of a lush and more diverse ecosystem of other coins and tokens, that are often regarded as cryptocurrencies in general, even when most of them do not fall under the definition of a "currency".

It cannot be tracked or regulated easily. Although all transactions are on the public ledger, there are steps to distance the user from the transaction, making Bitcoin transactions difficult to trace.

You do not have to trust organizations with your private details. To make an online transaction with a credit card, you have to give your credit card info, which contains your personal details. Those databases get hacked, and that puts your data at risk; it is possible for hackers to make fraudulent transactions with your credit card. With cryptocurrencies however, you never have to give anyone your private key thus keeping your personal details secure.

Unfortunately, this privacy also makes cryptocurrencies perfectly suited for criminal activity since anyone could buy or sell something without leaving a trail back to themselves. The private key keeps their personal information secret. Cryptocurrencies are widely used for transactions involving drugs, money laundering, and guns on the dark web.

How Does Cryptocurrency Work?

This is a very simplified flow, but here are the basics of how a transaction using cryptocurrency works.

Transacting with Cryptocurrency

Firstly a software wallet is obtained, which facilitates the buying, selling, and storage of coins.

When any quantity of a cryptocurrency is exchanged, the software wallets of the buyer and seller interact to produce a unique transaction ID, which goes into a pool of transactions that are pending.

Transactions in the pending pool of transactions need to go through the mining process to solve the cryptographic puzzle, before being added to the Blockchain.

Once a pending transaction is added to the Blockchain, it is basically permanent, and currency is considered to have changed hands.

Mining a Cryptocurrency

A user has the option to download the software that powers the peer-to-peer network onto their computer and use it to solve cryptographic puzzles in the pending transactions pool. The user is exchanging his computing power in exchange for cryptocurrency; this is known as mining.

As the currency matures, the mining becomes less lucrative as the cryptographic puzzles become more and more difficult. Users are more likely to simply trade their money for cryptocurrency in the hopes of it going up in value, or they may choose to invest in an Initial Coin Offering (ICO).

Categorization of Cryptocurrencies

When looking at investing in cryptocurrencies or ICOs, not all cryptocurrencies are the same. While coins and tokens are regarded as cryptocurrencies, there is a difference between the two.; Coins do not function as a currency or medium of exchange.

The term cryptocurrency is a misnomer since a currency technically represents a unit of account such as a dollar, a peso, or a pond. This is a store of value and a medium of exchange.

The naming comes from the fact that the characteristics of being a medium of exchange and a store of value are inherent within Bitcoin. And since the cryptocurrency space can trace its origins to Bitcoin's creation, any other coins conceived after Bitcoin is generally considered as a cryptocurrency although some do not fulfill the aforementioned characteristics of an actual currency.

The most common categorization of cryptocurrencies are:

- Alternative Cryptocurrency Coins (Altcoins)
- Tokens

The main difference between Altcoins and tokens is in their structure; Altcoins are separate currencies with their own separate Blockchain while tokens operate on top of a Blockchain that facilitates the creation of decentralized applications.

Altcoins

Alternative cryptocurrency coins are also called Altcoins or simply "coins". They are often referred to interchangeably as one or the other.

Altcoins simply refers to coins that are an alternative to Bitcoin since a number of Altcoins are a fork of the Bitcoin Blockchain, built using Bitcoin's open-sourced, original protocol with changes to its underlying codes.

This fork results in the creation of an entirely new cryptocurrency coin with a different set of rules and protocols. Examples of Altcoins that are variants of Bitcoins codes are Namecoin, Peercoin, Litecoin, Dogecoin, and Auroracoin.

There are also other Altcoins that did not originate from Bitcoin's open-source protocol. Rather, they have created their own Blockchain and protocol that supports their native currency. Examples of these coins include Ethereum, Ripple, Omni, Nxt, Waves and Counterparty.

A common feature of all Altcoins is that they each possess their own independent Blockchain, where transactions relating to that Altcoin are recorded.

Tokens

Tokens are a representation of a particular asset or utility, that usually resides on top of another Blockchain. Tokens can represent basically any assets that are fungible and tradable, from commodities to loyalty points to even other cryptocurrencies!

Creating tokens is a much easier process as you do not have to modify the codes from a particular protocol or create a Blockchain from scratch. Instead, a standard template on the Blockchain is used to create tokens. The Ethereum or Waves platform are two examples of this; Where the functionality of creating new tokens is made possible through the use of smart contracts or other innovations of Blockchain.

Tokens are created and distributed to the public through an Initial Coin Offering (ICO), which is a means of crowdfunding, through the release of a new cryptocurrency or token to fund project development. It is similar to an Initial Public Offering (IPO) for stocks, with critical distinctions which we will cover in a later chapter.

Types of Assets & Currencies

Historically, there are two types of money: precious metals and fiat currencies. Cryptocurrencies are a new, third type of currency that shares characteristics with both.

Precious Metals

Since trade was invented people have exchanged rare commodities as forms of value, as an alternative to barter trading which may not always work out. Any material that has scarcity and desirability is deemed to have value, and that can be divided into small amounts works for this purpose. Traditionally gold and silver are commonly used for this purpose.

While it is no longer practical to pay for goods in gold and silver, the main advantage of precious metals is that no government has control over their price and value. The value of gold and silver is inherent due to it being universally recognized and scarce. Investors view it as catastrophe-insurance because it will always have at least some form of value and offers protection against inflation, fraud, and economic collapse.

For these reasons, Bitcoin and other cryptocurrencies share some characteristics with precious metals. They serve as an asset class that may be partially uncorrelated with other types of assets and are popular among people that do not have a lot of trust in governments or the stability of the global economy, and of course other people that just want to financially speculate.

Fiat Currency

Dollars, pounds, yen, and all other currencies are "fiat currencies"; they have no intrinsic value other than the fact that a government has decreed that they are legal tender.

The United States dollar for example, has value because the United States government declares that it has value, and people have enough faith in the stability of that declaration to collectively agree with that decision.

Fiat currencies are much more convenient. It is easier to carry around a stack of bills rather than a bag of gold. However, it carries with it a different set of risks. When a government fails, its fiat currency typically hyper-inflates.

The Venezuelan Bolivar is a recent example, with the inflation rate estimated at over 4,000 percent in late 2017. In context, the standard inflation rate for most currencies is around 2 percent. Imagine if a loaf of bread that originally costs $1 doubles every few days! This phenomenon is theorized by economists to be caused by a country's negative reaction to their government's fiscal (monetary) policy, believing that their country is going into deficit.

Cryptocurrencies

Bitcoin was created to be a modern form of gold and it has been dubbed as "Digital Gold" by some online communities.

Powered by Blockchain technology, Bitcoin is decentralized and digital.

Decentralization means that the existence of Bitcoin is not linked to any individual entity. No government, bank, corporation, or individual "owns" the Bitcoin platform or has control over it.

Digital simply means that Bitcoin exists as data, and can be used for both online and offline applications with the right tools or applications. Because of this, it can be divided into small quantities similar to precious metals. It is possible to send fractions of a Bitcoin, with the smallest unit being a "Satoshi" which is 0.00000001 of a Bitcoin.

Pegged Cryptocurrencies

A pegged cryptocurrency sometimes referred to as a Smartcoin, is a cryptocurrency that has its value tied to that of another medium of exchange such as the currency of a country, like the US dollar, or a precious metal like gold. The exchange rate between the pegged cryptocurrency and the asset is arbitrarily determined as its inception, and its value fluctuates in a manner similar to the asset.

Unpegged cryptocurrencies are extremely volatile due to market perceptions, with the largest fluctuation being over 40% in December 2017. Pegged cryptocurrencies however, protect the asset from these turbulences in price. This requires the cryptocurrency project owners to hold a specific amount of that currency or precious metal in reserve at all times, ensuring that anyone holding that cryptocurrency is able to exchange it at the pegged rate at any time.

Chapter 3. Valuing Cryptocurrencies

When looking at investments, whether they are stocks, futures, or bonds, fundamental analysis is used to evaluate its value. This is done by examining related economic, and financial factors both qualitative and quantitative. Finding an investment with good financials and viability gives investors confidence that it is a risk worth taking. When looking at cryptocurrencies for investments however, is a whole different ball game as there are no financials to analyze.

Cryptocurrencies exist as code instead of a corporation, they are intended to represent value or assets on a network. Therefore the viability of a cryptocurrency is not based on the revenue it generates (because it is not a corporation), but rather it depends on the community that surrounds the cryptocurrency. The number of users that participate on the platform, use its services, mine or hash the algorithms are all part of the factors that determine the success or failure of a cryptocurrency.

To add further complexity in assessing the value of cryptocurrencies, they are all in the developing stage. Blockchain is a relatively new technology, and there have not been any wide scale adoption of the technology yet as of early 2018. Without any prominent use cases and real world examples, it makes it difficult to show a track record of what factors to look out for when assessing the profitability of an investment in cryptocurrency.

Still it is possible to make an informed guess. When assessing the fundamentals of cryptocurrencies the approach has to be different to take into account the uniqueness of Blockchain technology and the way it is revolutionizing the way we look at currencies and exchange of value. With the challenges laid out, you can understand why it is crucial that we research the viability and potential of each cryptocurrency independently and thoroughly before making a decision on whether to invest or not.

The Difficulty in Assessing the Value of a Cryptocurrency

Some analysts looking at cryptocurrencies have suggested that they are similar to commodities and should be assessed in a similar way. As there is no clear value of any commodity (such as precious metals), the price is determined by the market. Economics come into play, and the idea of demand and supply of the commodity play a role in determining its final price. However, it is the scarcity of the commodity that determines the range of where the price of the commodity sits. For example, the price per ounce for gold is over $1,200, while silver is at $15 approximately. That means an ounce of gold is worth almost a hundred times more than an ounce of silver.

On the surface, it does seem that there is a limitation to the number of a cryptocurrency that can be in circulation. The algorithm usually has a limit, which for Bitcoin is at 21 million. However, the number of cryptocurrencies that can exist is not limited in any way. As of May 2018, there are over 1,600 different cryptocurrencies with an estimated total market cap of $390 billion. Adoption of these currencies might vary by a huge amount, as there is a small handful with less than $1,000 in market cap.

Lastly, Cryptocurrencies are volatile, their market share is fickle, and updates and changes to the algorithm can result in split currencies. This has happened to Bitcoin in the past, with 19 forks recorded in 2017. Ethereum has also split into a fork called Ethereum Classic due to a difference in opinion on the technical direction of the Blockchain; this split is notable due to the estimated $264 million in value that was lost due to the split.

Factors Affecting the Value of a Cryptocurrency

Now that you have a clear idea of the challenges involved in evaluating a cryptocurrency asset, let us look at what does affect the value of coins. The fluctuations in the market from Bitcoin's meteoric rise to almost $20,000 and subsequent crash has to be explained in some way. I have summarized this in 3 simple points to look out for when assessing the value of a cryptocurrency.

1. Utility

Utility is simply the usefulness that a consumer gets from any good or service, it is basically the capacity of a good or service to give satisfaction.

In the case of a cryptocurrency, its utility is found in its ability to solve a problem. This utility incentivizes people to hold the cryptocurrency and is strongly correlated with its value.

For example, Ethereum's value is derived from its ability to allow developers to build and launch their own decentralized apps (dapps). Ethereum's currency ETH or Ether is used to execute transactions and development and as the demand the Ethereum Blockchain gains in popularity the demand for Ether increases, which in turn raises the price of the currency.

The utility of a coin is considered one of the most important factors to understand when valuing a cryptocurrency. The use case of the cryptocurrency and the issues that it addresses should be reflected in its price, otherwise, it is an indication that it is undervalued.

A coin without a well thought out use case is purely speculative in nature and does not provide any fundamental value. Avoid investing your money in these.

2. Economics

In economics, it is said that the value of any item in a marketplace is what people will pay for it. That, in turn, is determined by market forces which boils down to demand and supply. A cryptocurrency with a huge number available for sale, but with no one interested in buying will eventually have to lower its price or be left unsold. Conversely, a cryptocurrency with a larger number of buyers than sellers will see buyers increase their price as they clamor to get a piece of the action.

The other economic theory that affects the value of coins is the scarcity. A fixed supply of an item makes it scarce, which lowers the available supply. Bitcoins maximum of 21 million coins, for example, creates a ceiling on the supply. If there is utility associated with the cryptocurrency, demand will push up its price the closer we get to the 21 million cap for Bitcoin.

Mining difficulty indirectly causes scarcity as well. As the hash difficulty increases with the size of the Blockchain, it will take longer and longer to mine a unit of the cryptocurrency which reduces the supply of the cryptocurrency available in the market. Understanding how mining affects a particular cryptocurrency may require you to understand the technical details of the code, but it will surely be a key factor in determining the price of the cryptocurrency.

Sometimes artificial scarcity can also be created by employing a "burning" mechanism which destroys some coins. This is usually done for making new coins, for rewarding existing investors, or to destroy unsold coins after an ICO.

3. Market Sentiment

An extension of demand and supply, the market perception of the coin can affect its value. Projects that persistently achieve their milestones that were set out in their white paper may drive the price up due to the market perceiving this as the cryptocurrency succeeding in its goal.

Collaborations and partnerships with credible companies or other projects is a good sign of expansion. Such as when popular brands partner with a cryptocurrency or Blockchain company on a project. The support of popular brands boosts the visibility of the cryptocurrency and raises its value on the market.

Market sentiment can also affect the prices negatively as in the case of the Mt. Gox security breach in 2014. This caused Bitcoin prices to fall by 36% when the reports of approximately 850,000 Bitcoins were lost or stolen. The security breach caused the market to question the security of cryptocurrency exchanges, and affected investor confidence. This resulted in a drop in price, especially since Mt. Gox handled close to 70% of all Bitcoin transactions at the time.

Section 2: Investing - ICOs and Trading

Chapter 4. How ICOs Work

There is a huge trend for ICOs, with Blockchain investments totaling over $3.7 billion in 2017. In the first 3 months of 2018 alone ICOs raised more capital than the whole of 2018, and ICOs are expected to remain popular for some time to come.

Since many ICOs offer bonuses and the prices of their tokens rise once they hit the exchanges, ICOs are a very popular medium of investment for those interested to put their money in cryptocurrencies.

In this chapter, we will explore what ICOs are, and how they work and how they differ from traditional fundraising.

What is an ICO?

An initial coin offering (ICO) is an unregulated (by banks, government, or financial institutions) means of crowdfunding a project through the creation and sale of cryptocurrency. ICOs are mainly used by startups, and it is sometimes called an Initial Public Coin Offering.

When initiating an ICO, an amount of cryptocurrency is pre-allocated to investors in the form of tokens in exchange for other cryptocurrencies such as Bitcoin or Ethereum. Occasionally tokens are sold for cash as well. These tokens become functional units of cryptocurrency if the ICO's funding goal is met and the project launches.

While the primary purpose of an ICO is to generate funds for the company offering an ICO, it also attracts developer attention to the project and generates public awareness of the cryptocurrency. The aim is to increase the adoption and market share of the coin, and thereby the use of the company's Blockchain. This will increase the value of the cryptocurrency as the market perception of the ICO is popularized; having a large community is the key to the long term success of any cryptocurrency.

ICOs vs. IPO - What is the Difference?

The traditional way of raising funds is called an Initial Public Offering (IPO), and it is the public sales of the shares of the company. To understand ICOs, we will compare them with IPOs which differ in 4 main ways.

1. **Regulatory Oversight**

   IPO: A prospectus must be created by the company to declare it is intending to hold an IPO. There are standards for the prospectus and must include specific information such as the details of the company and its financials among other things.

   ICO: A whitepaper is created by the company to declare its intention to hold an ICO. There are no standards for this and the company may choose to include or exclude any information, or choose not to publish a whitepaper at all (although this is not recommended and raises red flags in investors).

   In July of 2017, the U.S. Securities and Exchange Commission (SEC) has started classifying ICO tokens as securities and are regulating them as such. While this does not affect investors, companies based in the United States are required to adhere to the SEC guidelines.

2. **Track Record & Credibility**

IPO: In order to hold an IPO, a company has a list of requires that it needs to meet such as having a minimum of at several million in pre-tax revenue, the exact amount varies according to regulations in each state, country, or stock exchange. The company also needs to demonstrate that it is solidly established with the proper systems in place that adhere to recognized business standards.

ICO: In contrast to this, ICOs are not held to any standards by any legal framework or organization. It is common and acceptable for companies to launch an ICO when they are still working on their proof of concept, which makes due diligence and financial assessment difficult if not outright impossible. The inherent risk should also be apparent, as there is no track record to forecast future earnings; instead you are investing in the future of the project based upon the ideas and vision of the company.

3. **Utility**

IPO: Investors in an IPO receive stock in the company from their investments. This represent a stake of ownership of the company, and may include voting rights in the company shareholder meetings. Some stock may also provide regular dividends.

ICO: Investors in an ICO do not own any share of the company or the project. Their investment grants them tokens which is a representation of value which correlates with its utility. Tokens may confer a stake in future earnings, or derive value from usage as we will explore later in this chapter.

4. **Timeframe**

IPO: Due to the legal requirements and the complexities that surround an IPO the entire process can take upwards of 6 months to complete.

ICO: In contrast the ICO process is considerably shorter in duration, and is dependent on the company or the project. The main consideration would be to give ample time to generate interest in the ICO through social media, advertising, or other channels. The fastest ICO was completed in 30 seconds and raised $36 million.

Why Do Companies Choose ICO?

ICOs allows a means for companies (mostly startups) to raise funds for their projects without the rigor of having to approach banks or venture capitals (VC) for funding. This also means that ICOs are a lower in cost as there is no need for regulatory compliance. When investing in ICOs, this will increase the risk as can be seen from a study done by Bitcoin.com. They found that 418 of the 902 ICOs (46%) listed on Tokendata for 2017, have failed in the first half of 2018, There are an additional 113 ICOs (13%) that are listed as "unresponsive", which could eventually result in being considered failed.

Building up the hype of the coin, especially since the cryptocurrency market is currently booming, is relatively easier and also has the benefit of generating interest in the company and the cryptocurrency. While this is essential to the success of the ICO, it also generates developer adoption and public awareness. As explained in an earlier chapter, this is crucial to the success of an ICO.

By going the ICO route for funding, the shares of the company do not change hands. This allows the owners or founders to keep the profits for themselves, or use the shares to raise additional funding at a later stage.

ICO Stages

An ICO is a huge undertaking and requires several steps by the company offering the ICO. Understanding these steps will help you to assess the ICO.

Announce the ICO: The company announces that it intends to hold an ICO to fund a project or service. This will raise attention to the communities that the announcement was made in, and generates interest in backing the project. The first impression that an ICO makes will play a huge role in determining its eventual success or failure.

Create and Publish the Whitepaper: The whitepaper details the plans for the ICO project and outlines the key points of the ICO. This includes the team members, the technical aspects, the legal issues, timeline, and potential risks of the project.

While white papers are intended to be a sales and marketing tool, it is typically written in an academic manner. It is a roadmap for the project, and attempts to justify the value of the cryptocurrency to investors by show casing its potential and features.

It is *mandatory* for all ICOs to have a whitepaper.

Get Advisors on Board the Project: Advisors lend credibility to a project, as well as provide experience to the company without the addition of another headcount. While they do not perform the functions of an employee, they are resources that are available to a company to help them achieve the goals of the project or resolve issues that may arise. There are 3 types of advisors that may lend their name to a project:

1. Advisor in Name

These advisors are there to provide credibility and publicity to a project, and are usually well known people.

2. Cryptocurrency/Blockchain Expert

These advisors bring experience on cryptocurrencies and Blockchain as the name implies. They would have prior experience with ICOs and their presence is there to ensure that the project has good governance and has a smooth launch.

3. Subject Matter Expert

These advisors are experienced in the project in aspects other than those related to cryptocurrencies or Blockchain. These advisors are usually brought in when a company is trying to bring Blockchain or cryptocurrencies to a different industries.

In all 3 cases, the more well known the advisor's profile is the more positively the ICO offering will be perceived by the market.

Conduct the ICO: An ICO will usually have a webpage and advertise on social media, as well as have a means to keep people who are interested in the project updated about developments and important updates. The ICO needs to be executed and are usually split into two stages; a pre-sale period and a public sale period.

1. Pre-Sale Period

This period is open only exclusively to a select group of people, individuals, or institutions. Buying the cryptocurrency during the pre-sale period usually awards a bonus amount of coins, and very commonly has a minimum purchase amount attached to it.

A pre-sale period is usually used to reward early adopters of the cryptocurrency, and guarantees them an amount of tokens to build up publicity. This allows the company to develop more of their product or service before the public ICO.

2. Public Sale Period

The public sale period is open to everyone who registers for the project and meet the KYC (Know Your Customer) compliance. KYC was put in place for cryptocurrencies to satisfy anti money laundering regulations.

Once the ICO has been successfully launched by reaching its funding goals, it will be listed on an exchange where the tokens be traded.

Develop the Product: When the ICO is complete, the company needs to carry out the plan laid out in the whitepaper. This means completing the development of the product or service, bring the team up to capacity, and get public adoption of the token. This will increase the value of the token by improving public perception, and keep investors happy.

Types of ICO Tokens

While there are two types of cryptocurrencies, tokens and coins, there are different categories of tokens from those with long term value, to those with a novelty. Identifying the value of a token by understanding its fundamentals is important.

Currency tokens are intended as a store of value and a medium of value exchange. Bitcoin is an example of a currency token.

Utility/asset tokens provides a service or a good in exchange for the token. It is a currency token, but also allows the token to be exchanged for a good or service. Ethereum is an example of a utility token. An asset token would be a token pegged to an asset such as Steem Dollar, which is pegged 19:1 to the US dollar.

Equity tokens gives partial equity or ownership of a company or organization. This sometimes gives control or voting rights as well. An example of an equity token is DAO. It is also known as a securities token as these tokens are subject to the SEC securities regulations.

Chapter 5. Doing your Due Diligence

Now that you understand what ICOs are, it is time for us to delve into the idea of investing in them. If you would like a refresher on the risks and difficulties of evaluating the value of cryptocurrencies, they are covered in Chapter 3.

Technical and Fundamental Analysis for Cryptocurrencies

When it comes to analyzing any investments (including cryptocurrencies) there are 2 main ways that to assess the value and risk of the investment.

Fundamental analysis assesses the value of a cryptocurrency by looking at the variables and metrics of the project to evaluate if it's a good investment from the bottom up. Very commonly discounted cash flow analysis, ratio valuation, or some other analysis method is used. But for cryptocurrencies, they do not generate cash flows, or pay dividends, or bear interest rates. Fundamental analysis also encompasses researching the whitepaper, the background of the advisors, social media, websites and other qualitative data relating to the cryptocurrency or ICO. In essence, fundamental analysis looks at the intrinsic value of a cryptocurrency by evaluating the economic variables and financials.

Technical analysis, on the other hand, looks at charts and histories to analyze and track trends. This includes a statistical analysis of market activity in order to predict the future price of the cryptocurrency. This methodology focuses more on quantitative data and does not attempt to measure the underlying value of the cryptocurrency. Instead technical analysis utilizes price charts and other indicators to identify patterns that can then be translated to actionable investment decisions.

Whatever your preferences are between fundamental and technical analysis, cryptocurrencies should not be analyzed with one methodology alone. Both technical analysis and fundamental analysis have to be taken into consideration to give context to the numbers.

Importance of Due Diligence

The idea of due diligence arose from IPOs, where it is a legal obligation to assess the credibility of the company undergoing an IPO. As ICOs have a higher risk than traditional IPOs, due diligence is even more vital to ensure that the company and project is thoroughly investigated prior to investing your hard earned money.

ICOs have a much higher risk than IPOs due to the fact that not only are the companies undergoing an ICO not profitable, most only have their product or service in the development stage. Due diligence ensures that the ICOs you invest in have strong fundamentals and will remain viable in the long term, which is important to reducing your risk.

In the next section, we will look at how to perform due diligence when considering to invest in an ICO.

How to Evaluate an ICO

In Chapter 4, we learned that ICOs differ from IPOs in that there is no track record. Instead ICOs are banking on future returns as very often their product or service is in development. Therefore, when doing your due diligence what you are trying to do is to identify factors that suggest stability and long term viability.

Whitepaper

The whitepaper is the most logical place to start, and if the company does not have one it is a huge red flag. Be sure to read it thoroughly.

The whitepaper should be comprehensive and in-depth. It should clearly define the technology and outline the roadmap for the project and their technology. If there are inconsistencies or any ambiguities, be very cautious.

Team

The first place to start the evaluation is the team. They are one of the most important criteria, if not the most important criteria, in determining the success or failure of the company.

When assessing the team, check their background and history, along with the skills and contributions that each member brings to the project. While their past performance is not a guarantee of future success, it can help you determine if they are in over their head, or if they have a reasonable chance of pulling off what they have laid out in their whitepaper.

Advisors

The importance of advisors are covered in Chapter 2, but should be evaluated in the same way as team members. Understanding their role in the project, and their background will give an indication of whether the advisors are adding value to the project, or are just there to generate hype (which in itself may not be a bad thing).

Partnerships

Partnerships bring a lot of value to the project as strategic partnerships can add credibility and publicity to the project. A reputable brand name that associates itself with a project is a signal that they are willing to bet their reputation on the project.

Competition

Understanding the market landscape will help you to understand what the company is up against, and what obstacles they will have to surmount to succeed. This also provides a reference point to understand how the project is different and how they are trying to disrupt the market if at all.

Blockchain Use Case

Blockchain is the basis of all cryptocurrencies, and hence the use of the Blockchain will determine the viability of the ICO. What you should be looking at here is whether the Blockchain is necessary for the use case, and what benefits it brings over the original method.

Developing a Blockchain is expensive and complex, and it opens up a lot of possible vulnerabilities in the security of the system. These are just as expensive to hunt down and fix, and makes the cost of the entire project a serious financial endeavor.

There has to be a unique value proposition to the use of Blockchain with a practical and quantifiable application. However, this also needs to be balanced with ease of use.

Planned Use of Funds

Understanding how the company plans to use the funds that are being raised will help you to understand how sound their strategies are, and assess the viability of their investment. This is most commonly found in the whitepaper, and should be carefully examined for any questionable expenditures.

Project Stage

How far along the development of the project will help investors in determining how viable the project is. If the project is in alpha, it might be worthwhile to check if there is a public version of it, and check the version history or even the code if you are technically inclined.

Also, it is common for projects to have a development plan for the project, and comparing what the company is committing to may be a way to assess the feasibility of the project.

Previous Funding and Capital Raised

Understanding of a company has any previous funding, and who the investors are is standard practice when going through an IPO. For an ICO, it is not common for companies to have raised capital prior to calling for an ICO. However, understanding their cash flow and if they have had prior funding can give some insight into who is backing the company, and if they have any liabilities or debts.

Token distribution

Understanding how the project intends to distribute the tokens from an ICO will indicate how the rewards will be split. This is similar to how equity is split in an IPO. If the company owners retain too many tokens, they are either very optimistic about the price or their funding goals are low. If it is the opposite situation, then there may not be enough incentive to ensure the project stays on track.

Not having enough tokens allocated to the company owners may be a red flag indicating the possibility of a scam.

Token Cap

An ICO may have a set cap limit on how much capital they intend to make. A hard cap will create scarcity in the tokens as there will be less coins in circulation. An uncapped ICO, also known as a soft cap, will collect as much as possible during the ICO to give the project team more funds to work with and spend on developing the project. As ICOs with open caps grow larger, there is less potential upside for investors.

A soft cap should have a minimum threshold in order to be considered a success.

Public Opinion

The cryptocurrency community has a lot of opinions, usually conflicting, on whether an ICO is a risk worth taking. While there is a lot of noise, but spending a little time sifting through it can uncover angles that you may be missing. The naysayers may also know something you do not.

Do a search on the ICO and see what comes up, but also check out what is being discussed on social media, and cryptocurrency forums.

Project Community

Check if the project has any forums or public chats such as Slack or Discord. An engaged community is a positive sign that the project is gaining adoption.

Additionally, noting the number of nodes that the project's Blockchain has is also a positive sign and shows the true popularity of the project.

Legal Risk

Understanding the legalities may be an uphill battle, especially since a lot of cryptocurrencies are operating independent of governments and banks. However, as companies are offering the ICOs, and investors are individuals subject to the law, there may be regulations that apply to you or your investment.

Additionally, there are countries beginning to impose regulations on ICOs, and fundraising could be hindered. This will affect the project and the company.

Chapter 6. ICO Red Flags

When looking at ICOs and their whitepaper, there is a lot of complicated computing terms due to the technical nature of cryptocurrencies and Blockchain. Add to that the fact that Blockchain is a relatively new technology, and there is an abundance of new and novel concepts with innovate uses springing forth as it gains traction.

The lack of regulations and understanding surrounding cryptocurrencies also further compound the issues as explained earlier. With the number of cryptocurrencies and tokens to choose from, it is tough to sieve out the genuine opportunities from the scams. And in the current environment where there are few check and balances, the cryptocurrency world is has an abundance of scammers. In April 2018, Techcrunch reported one company that disappeared with $660 million in raised capital from an ICO!

You can understand why you should be on alert for fraud, and how important it is to consider the red flags before investing is knowing when not to invest your money. There are certain unique traits of a cryptocurrency that includes decentralization, full transparency through a public ledger, and an open source code that is accessible by the public. It is common for scams not to have these traits and by watching out for them you will avoid a number of obvious traps.

Signs of Fraud

When investing your money in cryptocurrencies, the likelihood of recovering your assets in the event of fraud is almost nonexistent. Since there are little to no regulations on ICOs, there are almost no avenues of recourse.

Therefore, identifying the potential sings of ICO fraud is much more crucial then when you invest in other investment vehicles.

Red Flag 1: Unrealistic Offers

While it may be common to hear of incredible opportunities with high returns, there are ICOs that are now also offering daily or monthly returns of 180% or even higher. That sounds impractical as that means that the company would need to generate consistent profits from launch. Even with a working prototype, it will take some time for market acceptance of the Blockchain project and for the value of the cryptocurrency to rise.

Therefore, If there are "guaranteed" high returns and it looks too good to be true, then it is probably a scam.

There are generally 3 common schemes in the cryptocurrency community that promotes itself using unrealistic claims usually with a high incidence of fraud:

Cloud Mining Services

Cloud mining is a pooling of resources to mine cryptocurrency, as explained in Chapter 1. Profit here depends on the price of electricity, the computing power of the mining pool, as well as the hardware costs. The cloud mining company also takes a percentage of the cryptocurrency mined as a fee.

While not all cloud mining services are scams, it is risky as there are many ponzi schemes that disguise themselves as cloud mining companies.

There are also legitimate companies that operate cloud mining services and are labeled as scams when people lose the money they invested. This happens due to the volatility in the price of cryptocurrencies as it increases the risk of investment. In a bear market when prices are dropping, prices of electricity remain constant while the difficulty of hashing the cryptocurrency algorithm continues to increase which erodes to profitability of cloud mining.

Bitcoin Investment Packages (BIPs)

BIPs was popularized by USI Tech that offered a "guaranteed returns" for 140 days on the initial investment purchased. The claims from the executives of USI are based on math as they have been known for operating a trading automation algorithm and giving advice in the foreign exchange (Forex) market.

In December 2017 the Texas State Securities Board issued an emergency cease and desist to USI Tech, and they have since shutdown sales and marketing operations as of January 2018. While there are many allegations, it is not clearly stated if USI Tech was indeed a scam. Also, it seems that investment platforms are at the very least against the regulations of the securities board of certain states.

In general BIPs promise high-yield on investment with high regular payouts. They are characterized by using complex jargon and marketing buzzwords, or sometimes advanced mathematics and unnecessary algorithms to confuse or bedazzle investors and add to their credibility.

BIPs have a life cycle where profit will be paid out to early investors, and to entice more investment in their scheme. Typically they would shut down once the intake of users starts to dwindle as the influx of funds slows. That is when the founders will shut down the company and disappear with the money, leaving the last batch of investors bearing a loss.

Unsolicited Offers and Pressure Tactics

If the ICO offer is unsolicited or you have been "prequalified" be wary, especially if you are not actively participating in the cryptocurrency forums and social media. These unsolicited ICOs are similar to the scam emails that prey on the uninformed by playing on their greed. Reputable ICO projects have sufficient avenues to generate publicity and gain a following without the need to resort to unsolicited emails.

These emails may also include limited time offers or exclusive bonuses only via an email link. Be especially wary if you do not recognize the sender.

Red Flag 2: "Cryptocurrencies" Lacking the 3 Basic Criteria

These three basic criteria are what defines a cryptocurrency. If an ICO is missing these three criteria, it is not a cryptocurrency running on a Blockchain being offered. It is very likely a scam in this case.

Code Base Is Not Open Source

All cryptocurrencies are running on Blockchain technology, and due to their decentralized nature their code is always open source. That means that any member of the public has access to the code. Being open source allows anyone to look at the code and review it to suggest improvements. The code for cryptocurrencies are usually found at Github.

Ledger Is Not Decentralized

A Blockchain ledger is always decentralized, meaning that the ledger is stored on multiple nodes. This makes it impossible for anyone to tamper with transaction histories. If a cryptocurrency is not decentralized, then it is not running on Blockchain technology and is not a cryptocurrency by definition.

Tokens Are Not Awarded for Mining

Tokens are always awarded by mining, regardless of which "proof" system the Blockchain version uses, there must be a private key, a public key, and a hash. If tokens are not awarded to miners, then it does not have a means to motivate people to use their computing power to solve the cryptographic hash.

Red Flag 3: Use Case Does Not Require Blockchain

While Blockchain is integral to cryptocurrencies, there are projects with a legitimate Blockchain but may still raise a red flag. This happens when Blockchain is unnecessarily or incorrectly applied.

The purpose of Blockchain and the cryptographic algorithms surround it was originally designed to keep the identities and the transactions between users private. If there is no need for this level of privacy, a secure server would suffice.

While not a scam in any sense of the word, an unnecessary application of Blockchain technology will complicate an existing process or product instead of disrupting the industry. Their use of Blockchain and mining will eventually result in inefficiencies instead of adding value.

Even if the ICO succeeds, the project may eventually lose out to a company or product that is using more appropriate solutions that are able to be more cost effective.

Red Flag 4: Key Information is Not Available

As covered in Chapter 2, the whitepaper, team members and roadmap are important to evaluate the viability of the project as well as to justify the ICO. If these key pieces of information are missing, you may want to reconsider investing.

No White Paper

The whitepaper of an ICO should detail the technical details, team members, use of funds and other details of the project. It should justify the need for the project and is currently the accepted means of how investors benchmark an ICO since there is no historical performance or working product to evaluate.

If there is no whitepaper, it is a huge red flag.

Team Members or Advisors with Questionable Background

The team members' experience play a large part in determining the success or failure of a project. If you are not able to evaluate for yourself if the team behind the project is able to pull of what they set out to achieve as stated in the whitepaper, then you are going in blind.

Even if the details of the team are present, perhaps the most important to take note of are the number of developers and their background. Blockchain and cryptocurrency may be relatively new, but not having any prior experience or domain knowledge signals a high likelihood of failure.

Advisors on the project should also be evaluated the same way.

Unclear or Missing Roadmap

ICO projects typically list their funding and development goals with clear timelines. If this is ambiguous, or worse not stated at all, then even if the project is not a scam it may be doomed to failure.

Note that scammers may also create a roadmap and regularly falsify updates, so the existence of a roadmap does not automatically disqualify a project from being a scam.

Red Flag 5: No Public Discussion

A legitimate ICO project will want to communicate with investors and encourage discussion about their project to gain market acceptance and adoption. It is common for such projects to have public chats and forums, and you can often find their developers and other people interacting with members of the public through various forums, posts, and social media.

If an ICO project does not have any form of chat channel such as Slack or Telegram, and comments are turned off on their videos or social media posts there may be something that the company is trying to hide. In such cases, you may want to check with independent forums and evaluate the ICO project from a more objective viewpoint.

Chapter 7: Trading Cryptocurrencies

Now that we have covered ICOs, we need to look at how we can get in on the action. For this, we will need to understand how to buy and sell cryptocurrencies.

Similar to any other fiat currency there are exchanges where you can exchange your dollars, Pounds, Euros, or any other currency for that matter, for whatever cryptocurrency that the exchange is trading. This is similar to Forex or foreign exchange currency trading, where you identify and leverage on opportunities in the market.

The only difference is that these currencies are cryptocurrencies, and the exchanges are all online.

There are several steps that need to be taken before you can invest in an ICO or trade cryptocurrencies:

1. Pick an exchange to use
2. Set up a cryptocurrency wallet
3. Pick a cryptocurrency to trade

Exchanges

There are two types of exchanges, the first is a regular exchange where buyers and sellers put in orders with their prices. The exchange then matches the orders by price and then processes the trade. The second is a peer to peer exchange, which matches the users directly allowing the two parties to deal without an intermediary.

Regardless of which type of exchange you use cryptocurrency exchanges do not operate under any rules or regulations. Remember the case of Mt. Gox? They were one of the first to go mainstream, and they ended in bankruptcy. 24,000 customers around the world lost their investments totaling up to an estimated several hundred of millions of dollars.

The above example should illustrate why picking an exchange may seem like a simple task but with over 190 exchanges in existence it adds to the complexity of the many things to consider when making your choice.

Ease of use and security are valid concerns, and if you are investing a large sum of money it would make sense to prioritize this. In fact, this would be the primary concern of most investors but not the only ones.

Low transaction fees are another concern, but this will most likely result in trading on a newer, less established exchange. The risks involved here would be the lack of reputation, and the possible exposure to a scam or risk of having your money stolen in a hack. The recommendation from experts is to trade on a US based exchange, especially if you are based in the US.

Anonymity is another concern of traders, and going outside the US to trade would also mean more anonymity since there may not be a requirement for ID verification.

There are also exchanges that provide a one stop solution, offering an exchange and a wallet together. This is a good starting point for most beginners, and Coinbase is a good example of such an exchange with a good reputation.

Cryptocurrency Wallets

After choosing an exchange, the next step would be to set up a wallet. A wallet is a software program that stores private and public keys. These keys are needed to interact with the Blockchain to send and receive cryptocurrency.

Note that the currency itself is stored via transaction data in the Blockchain, only the private and public keys are stored in the wallet. As long as you have your private key and public key, you can access the Blockchain and your cryptocurrency. Without the keys, anything on the Blockchain is inaccessible. Once you lose your private key it is locked away for good in the Blockchain. Similarly, if someone uses your private key to transfer your cryptocurrency to their own account, it is impossible to recover.

Wallets are designed to hide your private keys from others, ensuring that only you have access to your cryptocurrency.

So what are the options of keeping your cryptocurrency safe? There are several types of wallets but generally they fall into two main categories of being online ("hot" wallets) or offline ("cold" wallets). As suggested by the name, online wallets store your private key on an online server where it is put at risk of being accessed by hackers. An offline wallet is stored in a manner that cannot be accessed online, such as storing your key on a USB drive or a hardware wallet.

A good practice is to spread your cryptocurrencies over several wallets, thereby preventing you from losing all your investments if a wallet is compromised or if you lose one of your keys. Commonly, online wallets are used for cryptocurrencies that are being actively traded, or those that you intend to flip. Offline wallets are used for those that you "hodl". If you store large amounts of cryptocurrency in an offline wallet, treat it like a brick of gold as it is probably as valuable as one, if not more.

Generally, expert advice agree that a hardware wallet is the choice for all investments and it is the best option to keep your cryptocurrency secure.

Types of Wallets

Hopefully, the you are convinced of the importance of securing your investment. Even if you intend to have an online wallet it is a good practice to secure some of your investments in an offline wallet. However, there are several different types of offline wallets as well from mobile apps to hardware each with their own features.

When choosing the type of offline wallets to use, you need to consider the physical as well as software security of the gadget, as well as how mobile or portable it is. It may be convenient to link your wallet to your mobile phone, but if your investment is sizable it may make more sense to have a wallet you can keep in a safe.

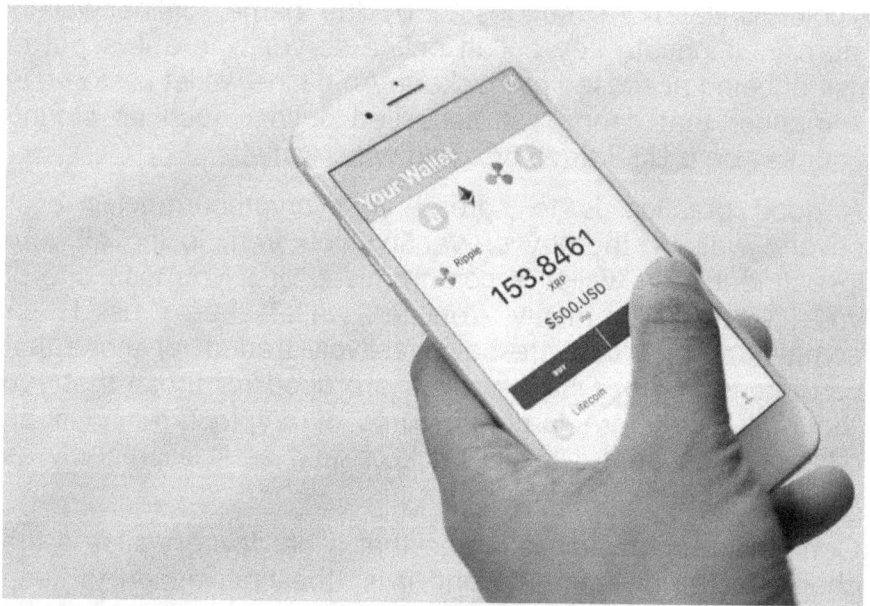

Mobile Wallets

A mobile wallet is simply app on for the phone. Many online wallets also offer the option for you to go mobile, with some of these online wallets storing your private key on your phone, but with an online encrypted backup in case your phone is lost.

These are the best option for people who would like to use cryptocurrency as a replacement for fiat currency. Similar to how Apple, Google, and Samsung use near-field communication (NFC) technology to pay for goods and services, hardware wallets allow you the same convenience with your cryptocurrency.

When choosing a mobile wallet, consider the types of cryptocurrency that you intend to store. If you are investing and trading in Bitcoin and Altcoins, then it may be a good option. If you are investing in Ether, Ripple or other coins, these are not as widely accepted as payment options as of the writing of this book. It may make more sense to go for another option.

Of course the phone's operating system (Android or iPhone mainly) will also play a part in your choice of mobile wallet. Due to the open platform that Android employs, there may be more options for wallets but there may also be more risk as malware is easier to sneak on to your phone. This may come in the form of emails, links, or even social media posts.

Desktop Wallets

Desktop wallets exist as an app on your desktop (or laptop). They originated when Bitcoin was new and mining software created the wallet for new miners. While most desktops are considered online wallets, it is possible to make them offline by creating what is known as an "air gap".

While they are more secure than mobile wallets as desktops are harder to steal, they are notoriously susceptible to malware since being a "hot" wallet puts them on the internet.

Similar to mobile wallets, desktop wallets should be evaluated with your needs of security and convenience in mind.

Hardware Wallets

Hardware wallets are devices that are small enough to fit in your pocket, and when needed, can be plugged into an internet connected computer to send or receive cryptocurrency. The basic idea behind it is that your private key is stored on this encrypted device that is seldom connected to the internet.

Hardware wallets also employ two factor authentication (2FA) which will require you to provide a PIN to access the wallet. While the most secure of the options as it provides enhance security against theft or scams, it is also the most expensive with prices around $100.

You could get a wallet for free by downloading a mobile or desktop app, but it is your investment at stake. While there have been reports of mobile and desktop wallets being hacked, there has not been a known case where this has happened to a hardware wallet.

Remember that once you lose your cryptocurrency it cannot be recovered.

Paper Wallets

Yes, you read that right. Paper wallets are basically a piece of paper with your private key written on it. While this is the most secure, remember that ink can fade, and paper can wear down over time, get lost in a stack of other documents, or worse get thrown away.

However, paper wallets will never get hacked as they cannot be connected to the internet.

Picking a Cryptocurrency

After picking an exchange to use and setting up your wallet, you are now able to trade in cryptocurrency. You will need to choose which cryptocurrencies to invest in and the two fundamental, most stable coins are Bitcoin and Ether (the currency of the Ethereum platform).

They are the usual entry point for investors new to cryptocurrency, and can be later traded for other cryptocurrencies or used in an ICO. This works to diversify your portfolio as other cryptocurrencies may increase or decrease their value independent of your initial investment.

Bitcoin has the advantage of being the first cryptocurrency, and therefore has widespread popularity. It is used for a wide variety of cryptocurrency payment solutions and is gaining in acceptance in retail as well as online stores.

Ether is not just a cryptocurrency, it is a token that can be exchanged to execute smart contracts. The Ethereum Virtual Machine (EVM) allows developers to build on top of the Ethereum Blockchain, thus granting Ether additional utility which translates into the value of Ether reflected in its price. Since Ethereum is a stable and convenient platform for Blockchain, Ethereum is a popular choice for companies going through an ICO.

Remember that no matter which cryptocurrency you invest in, it is extremely volatile and you should do your due diligence and invest with a strategy.

Chapter 8. ICO Investing Strategy

In this chapter, we look at a number of possible strategies you can adopt when selecting and investing in cryptocurrencies.

When investing at the ICO stage, your investment may generate ten times the amount of capital put in, while others may double or triple the principal sum. The question then is "how much should I be looking at?"

To give some figures, Mangrove Capital Partners, a Venture Capital firm headquartered in Luxembourg, has averaged 232 ICOs to give an average return of 13.2 times. That is a 1,320% return on every dollar, in contrast the Standard & Poor (S&P) Index's average of 10%.

If you are trading, the investments may be significant but not as jaw dropping. The figures for trading vary much more as it depends on your strategies, the state of the market, and the timing of your investments.

When making any investment, having an exit strategy is important especially more so with cryptocurrencies due to the complexities and risks involved. An exit strategy is a plan to be executed once certain predetermined criteria are met, or have been exceeded. A good exit strategy should also be a contingency against loss when an investment is not performing as expected, or if there has been a change in the market conditions.

This will keep you from second guessing yourself, or stress yourself out over decisions like whether you should hold the investments or cash out.

Things to Keep In Mind When Investing

When developing your own investing strategy, you should keep in mind these considerations as cryptocurrencies are highly volatile and speculative. Market conditions are changing and evolving with new developments, and regulations are being put into place by governments around the world. New investors entering the market also improves the liquidity and the number of trades, which skews data.

Due to these factors, there is no sureties in cryptocurrencies trading and ICO investing. Take all advice and opinions with a pinch of salt.

Cryptocurrency Valuation is Developing Slowly

As we learned in Chapter 3, there are factors such as utility, economics, and market sentiment that drive the value of cryptocurrencies. However, new models are constantly being developed and tested in this field. Valuation models will be eventually fine tuned, but until then we are living in a time of imperfect information.

While this presents risks as we are investing semi-blind at least, there are possible opportunities as well since there is a potential of certain cryptocurrencies being undervalued.

What Goes Up, Must Come Down

While the cryptocurrency has grown by over 3000% in 2017, it is expected that it will eventually crash. While Jim Newsome, the ex Commodity Futures Trading Commission Chair believes that this will not happen for some time to come, certain cryptocurrencies (like Bitcoin) have already crashed as can be seen at the end of 2017.

In the meantime, cryptocurrencies will certainly rise and fall several times and "flash crashes" can happen. A flash crash is when a withdrawal or cashing out of a cryptocurrency amplifies a price decline. That brings us to our next point...

Cryptocurrencies Are Volatile

While cryptocurrencies provide a lot of opportunities, and Blockchain is opening up possibilities of disruption in several markets, volatility is driven by investor perception. The market movement in cryptocrurencies may rise or fall by half, or even double in a single day. Compare this to a more traditional stock market, where anything close to 10% would cause a panic and you will understand why investors are considering this a high risk proposition.

This volatility is expected to stabilize as regulations are put in place, and the security of the Blockchain protocols are developed and security breaches are less common.

With that in mind, let us move on to a few strategies you can consider when investing in cryptocurrencies.

Strategy 1: Diversify Investments

Diversifying investments is a way of mitigating the risk of investing, as well as to capture various growth opportunities. In traditional investment vehicles like stocks, bonds, and other assets it is common to not put all your eggs in one basket. This is especially so when dealing with cryptocurrencies as the risk and volatility is much higher.

In the past it would have been acceptable and even profitable to go all in on a single cryptocurrency. However, with the Ethereum Enterprise Alliance (EEA), Blockchain technology is being further developed. This has resulted in Blockchain gaining a foothold in multinational corporations such as IBM and Intel. This presents the opportunity to leverage on Ethereum to diversify into other cryptocurrencies on the EEA.

Strategy 2: Invest for Bonus Offerings

Since most ICOs offer bonuses, it would make sense to take advantage of it where possible. Most commonly a bonus is awarded to early investors, with more tokens being awarded the earlier you invest. There are also bonuses being offered for referrals or with a certain sum invested.

If you are looking to invest, look for bonus offerings as it will increase your overall returns.

Strategy 3: Invest in Low Token Caps ICOs

A token cap (Chapter 5) refers to the maximum amount raised by the project, and creates scarcity since there are less coins in circulation.

At the ICO stage, a low token cap may result in the ICO being sold out more quickly but since demand is high the value will be more likely to increase. When trading a low token cap cryptocurrency, prices tend to be higher as demand will usually exceed the supply.

The scarcity of low token cap ICOs will make it difficult to get tokens, but if you do your gains will be greater if the token gains traction.

Strategy 4: Quick Flip Your Cryptocurrencies

A quick flip usually happens when you buy a cryptocurrency expecting it will increase in value in a short amount of time. The idea here is to make a fast profit then exit since the biggest gains usually occur not too long after purchase.

This usually happens from the hype when tokens from an ICO hit the market. By using the strategy of getting bonus tokens, it is also possible to recover your initial investment and then keep the rest as profit to be taken out at a later date. This eliminates your risk once you flip your tokens, and allows you to recycle your investment into other ICOs or another investment vehicle altogether.

The downside to this is that you will lose out on potential profits if you cash out before a bull run, and in some cases there are tokens with a lock in period where sales cannot take place. It is important that you weigh the long term and short term prospects of the project yourself and decide if this is a good strategy to use with your investment.

Breakthroughs in the Blockchain platform, found by paying attention to the fundamentals, can also be a signal that a flip may be a strategy to employ. These developments will be viewed positively by the market, and when it catches on will drive the prices of the affected cryptocurrencies up. Flipping tokens when trading usually focuses on Altcoins (Chapter 2), which are forks of the Bitcoin Blockchain. Therefore it makes sense to pay attention to the movements in Bitcoin as well when flipping.

Strategy 5: Hold the Tokens

A hold or "hodl" strategy indicates that you believe that your tokens will be profitable one day (if not currently profitable), or will increase in value compared to what it is today. This is best used when you are able to get tokens as cheap as possible, or you believe that the ICO has huge long term potential.

This is generally true as cryptocurrencies are still considered in the nascent stage with untapped potential. You need to be confident of your research (Chapter 5) in the project, the company, and believe in their vision and roadmap to employ this strategy.

Section 3: Looking to the Future

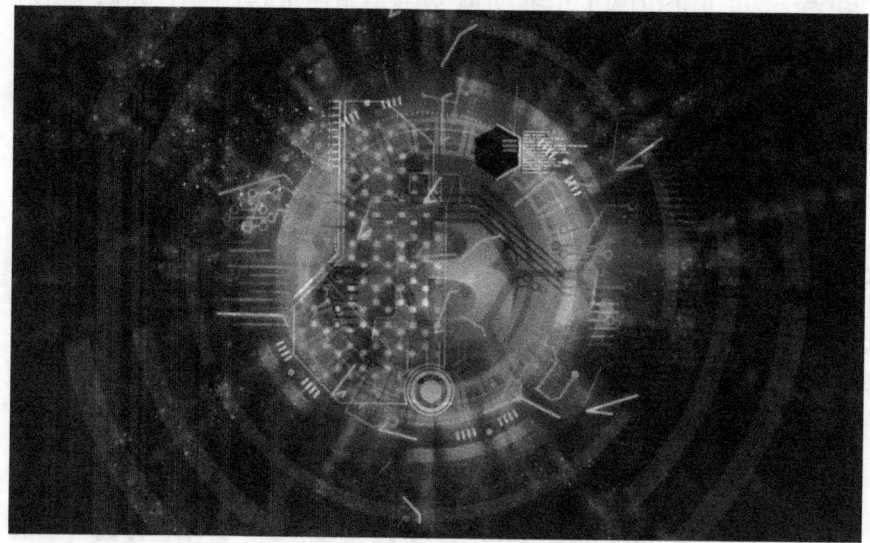

Chapter 9. The Future of ICOs

The future of the ICOs is likely to shape the future of the Blockchain; Disruption will happen as Blockchain continues to gain in acceptance, and cryptocurrencies are currently the main source of funding these projects.

Here are a few thoughts on the possibilities of the future of ICOs:

Trend 1: Increase in Scams

It is estimated that an average of $9 million in cryptocurrencies is lost every day to scams. Generally there are two types of scams, those centering around ICOs, and those centering around getting an individual's wallet information.

The fact that there are over 1,500 cryptocurrencies on exchanges suggests that there are at least that many ICOs that have taken place and with the rise of their popularity there will inevitably be an increase in scammers or poorly thought out projects hoping to ride the wave. Given that ICOs are not guaranteed and there is huge uncertainty when investing in cryptocurrencies there are many scams masquerading as ICO projects.

These fake ICOs may not be immediately evident as a scam, with some ponzi schemes launching successfully and only winding up operations when served with a cease and desist order. These can be avoided by doing your due diligence before investing.

Aside from fake ICOs, the cryptocurrency space is filled with phishing, fraud, theft and hacking as well. With the increase in popularity in cryptocurrencies it is no longer the exclusive domain of the tech community. There are a lot more people investing their money now or hoping to get rich quick. These people are less likely to be aware of security issues and as the popularity of cryptocurrencies rise, so will the number of scams.

Phishing, fraud, and theft prey on the ignorance, fear, and greed of people. Being informed of your rights, how the Blockchain works, and what are the best practices with regards to security can easily mitigate most of these risks.

Trend 2: Regulation Will Continue to Increase

ICOs and cryptocurrencies are becoming an area of focus for regulators around the world. In an attempt to curb money laundering, scams, and other undesirable behavior. Regulations are being put in place in various countries, each with their own approach. For more information, see the Chapter 10 for more information on regulation.

Most regulations being put in place centers around Know Your Customer (KYC) and Anti Money Laundering (AML) regulations in an attempt to curb illegal activity. However, there are regulations that are being put in place with regards to securities and cryptocurrencies as well. See Chapter 10 for more information about regulation.

Trend 3: Regulation will result in Securities Tokens

Securities Tokens will gain in popularity as regulators step in to scrutinize the cryptocurrency market. Securities Tokens embed regulatory requirements into tradable tokens and are backed by assets, profits, or revenue of a company giving it a tangible value from launch.

Investors in securities tokens must be authorized and verified to meet the criteria for each particular security token, thus providing assurance that the token is not vulnerable to manipulation.

While it was never intended for ICO tokens to be securities, the SEC has considered almost every ICO token as a security since it increases in value over time depending on the performance of the company.

The advantage of being a security is that this will add legitimacy to the ICO as scams will very unlikely want to comply with regulatory framework. This reduces the legal risk of the company and protects the investor and the company under securities law.

The disadvantage of this is the belief that once a token has been deemed a security, regulations and restrictions are imposed which can severely limit a project's ability to create a widely adopted platform that is necessary for its success.

Since the SEC crackdowns on token offerings in 2017, many ICOs have been trying to avoid having their tokens classified as securities.

Trend 4: VCs and Blockchain Will Fuel Each Other's Growth

As regulations are put in place and ICOs become even more publically accepted it will enable companies to be more liquid by converting their equity to cryptocurrency. While ICOs were originally disrupting Venture Capitals (VCs), funding in Blockchain companies have seen a surge in early 2018. As VC funds are pumped in, Blockchain projects will see a rise in popularity.

When VCs invest in an early stage company, capital is generally locked up for at least 5 years, with the possibility of a large payoff in the future. However, for Blockchain investments the return on a VC's investment could be as soon as a year. When the VC backed Blockchain projects start to show returns, investor confidence will rise and spur other VCs to invest as well.

The relationship between VCs and Blockchain will be best capitalized by those that are creating new business models where innovative ideas and new platforms can be developed. These projects can best leverage on the funds to create value and new ecosystems.

Trend 5: Platforms Will Further Develop

Platforms and infrastructure projects such as Ethereum will develop as projects are launched. The thing about these platforms is that even if the decentralized platforms fail, the developments as a result from the project will remain as a foundation for future projects.

As there are currently over 900 decentralized applications on Ethereum, we can reasonably expect that there will be new developments in the platform which will further evolve the tokenization of assets, smart contracts, proof of stake, or any of the other elements of the Ethereum platform to improve its capabilities.

New platforms are also expected to arise to address the issues with the current platforms. These new platforms can be expected to improve on smart contract functionality, interoperability, scalability, and customization if they succeed and gain acceptance.

Trend 6: Hard Forks Will Happen as Ideals Clash

There are times when the power users of a cryptocurrency may collectively agree to split the Blockchain which will result in what is known as a hard fork. While there may be some people who believe that the Blockchain should not be altered, there are enough users who would want to "roll back" the block to a certain point in time.

This has occurred with both Bitcoin and Ethereum.

When Ethereum forked in June 2016, which resulted in Ethereum and Ethereum Classic, it was due to a hack that compromised the security of the system. One version of the Blockchain retains the records of a theft which came up to $50 million in value, while the fork rolled back the Blockchain to a point before the hack occurred.

Bit forked in August 2017 to create Bitcoin Cash due to bottleneck in the block size. As the Blockchain originally had a limit of one megabyte (1 MB) per block, the current size of the blocks were slowing down transactions for hours or even days. This fork allowed developers to adjust the block size to eight megabytes (8 MB).

In both these cases, uncertainty over which is the version of the cryptocurrency to back, as well as which ideology is better for the cryptocurrency results in price fluctuations.

Developers may also fork cryptocurrencies to raise funds. While technically not an ICO, a cryptocurrency that forks tend to fluctuate in value. If a cryptocurrency you invested in forks, you could stand to be affected if caught on the wrong side.

Chapter 10: Regulating Cryptocurrencies

While governments across the world are regulating or banning cryptocurrencies, the effects have yet to show any real effect on slowing the growth or popularity of cryptocurrencies. There has also been a push for self regulation to reduce the intervention from governments.

Self Regulation

Self regulatory bodies set standards as to what is appropriate and effective with regards to regulation. In this way they serve as a benchmark to educate and inform government regulators on how to model their policies and institute measure to protect their countries and citizens in a way that does not affect the long term growth and sustainability of cryptocurrencies.

The Digital Asset and Blockchain Foundation of India (DABFI) was formed in February of 2017 when a few cryptocurrencies appointed international law firm Nishith Desai Associates to develop regulations for cryptocurrencies which DABFI then presented to the Indian government.

CryptoUK was formed in 2018 to represent the interest of the cryptocurrency sector and are working on developing regulation in the UK, as well as a self regulatory framework for ICOs. The drive for regulation is spurred by wanting to ensure better due diligence against illegal activities, and securing their customer's funds and assets by protecting against hackers. They are also working preventing money laundering.

Sixteen government registered cryptocurrency exchanges in Japan have also formed a self regulatory body after the Coincheck hack that occurred in 2018, where over $530 million were taken by hackers.

Where Cryptocurrenices are Banned

Currently there are two countries in the world that have outright banned cryptocurrency trading and ICOs.

China

China has banned all ICO activities in 2017 and ordered cryptocurrency exchanges to shut down. The People's Bank of China banned has banned ICOs for all businesses and individuals. Chinese ICOs that have completed their funding cycles have been requested to refund any tokens raised. The People's Bank of China has also indicated it will investigate any company or individual found to be in violation of its ruling.

South Korea

Following the lead of China, South Korea's Financial Services Commission announced in September 2017 the prohibition of ICOs.

Other Regulations Around the World

The rest of the world have allowed trading in cryptocurrencies and ICOs, with differing levels of regulation depending on the country and region.

United States of America

ICOs are regulated in the United States, and the regulations vary widely from state to state. On the federal level, ICOs are expected to be registered and licensed the same as if they were regular investments. This includes registering with the Securities and Exchange Commission if the ICO is to sell or trade securities. Companies undergoing ICOs are also expected to adhere to anti money laundering (AML) and know your customer (KTC) practices.

United Kingdom

ICOs are allowed in the UK but the Financial Conduct Authority (FCA) has issued warning to investors stating that ICO projects are still experimental and therefore pose risks to investors. The FCA has stated that securities law and other areas of financial or banking law may apply to the issuance of a token depending on the different aspects and rights the token holder obtains through holding it.

European Union

ICOs are allowed in the European Union, provided they are in adherence to AML and KYC policies as well as required business regulations and licenses, according to the ICO company's business function.

Abu Dhabi

The Financial Services Regulatory Authority (FSRA) of the Emirate of Abu-Dhabi digital currencies are "commodities" and the majority of ICOs will be regulated as "specified investments." Tokens that are classified as "specified investments" (securities, shares, and bonds) and therefore fall under the FSMR regulation. The FSRA will determine whether a given ICO is subject to regulation on a case-by-case basis.

Australia

Australia allows ICOs and cryptocurrency trading, but requires disclosures if a cryptocurrency or an ICO falls under the Corporations Act. This happens if the ICO is a Managed Investment Scheme (MIS), or if the ICO is being offered as a share of a company, as a directive, or as a non-cash payment.

Canada

Canada allows ICOs and cryptocurrency trading, but they may need to be registered as securities. The Canadian Securities Administration stated that "[A] coin/token may still be a 'security' as defined in securities legislation of the jurisdictions of Canada. Businesses should complete an analysis on whether a security is involved."

Estonia

Estonia allows ICOs and cryptocurrency trading. Additionally the government is even considering conducting its own token sale to raise funds. However, the Eurozone rule on nation states not having their own currencies continues to split opinions about the possibility of this happening.

Germany

Germany allows ICOs and cryptocurrency trading. Regulation applicable to a token is dependent of the rights the cryptocurrency holds. An ICO may need to comply with current regulations including the Banking Act, Investment Act, Securities Trading Act, Payment Services Supervision Act, and Prospectus Acts.

Gibraltar

Gibraltar allows ICOs and cryptocurrency trading. In October 2017, the government established a framework for regulating distributed ledger technology companies, which came into offer in 2018. It encompasses ICOs and subjects them to financial controls and standards.

Hong Kong

Hong Kong allows ICOs and cryptocurrency trading. However, regulators have stated that certain tokens might be securities and should be treated as such.

Isle of Man

The Isle of Man allows ICOs and cryptocurrency trading. The country is working on a regulatory framework as of the early 2018, there is no schedule on its release.

Israel

Israel allows ICOs and cryptocurrency trading. However, the Israeli Securities Authority has announced that a panel was put in place to study how ICOs operate in the country. Israel also plans to introduce tax laws on ICO tokens and released earlier in 2018 a draft circular detailing how domestic ICOs could be taxed.

Japan

Japan allows ICOs and cryptocurrency trading. The Financial Services Authority made an announcement in 2017 that depending on the structure used, ICOs may be regulated under Japanese law, including by the Payment Services Act and the Financial Instruments and Exchange Act. Additionally the law requires cryptocurrency exchanges to hold a special license to operate in Japan.

Liechtenstein

Lichtenstein allows ICOs and cryptocurrency trading, but depending on the rights attached to a certain token, applicability of securities and financial instrument law may apply.

Lithuania

Lithuania allows ICOs and cryptocurrency trading. In some cases, current laws surrounding securities and money laundering may apply.

Philippines

Philippines allows ICOs and cryptocurrency trading but regulators have said that some tokens might be considered as securities and thus must comply with securities registration regulations. The Philippines Securities and Exchange Commission is currently working on regulations for cryptocurrency transactions.

Russia

Russia allows ICOs and cryptocurrency trading, but the government is working on a regulatory framework. Russia has stated that securities laws may apply to ICOs and has required cryptocurrency miners registration and taxation. Russia's government ministries proposed a law in early 2018 that, if approved, would introduce a capital requirement for ICO organizers.

Singapore

Singapore allows ICOs and cryptocurrency trading. The Monetary Authority of Singapore (MAS) released guidelines regarding cryptocurrencies and ICOs in 2017 classifying cryptocurrencies that are "capital market products" under the Securities and Futures Act. Therefore putting them under the regulation of the MAS. This includes cryptocurrencies that either infer an ownership interest in a corporation or product, debt, or a share in an investment scheme.

Switzerland

Switzerland allows ICOs and cryptocurrency trading, and is covered by money laundering, banking, securities and collective investment laws. The Swiss Financial Market Supervisory Authority (FINMA) released ICO guidelines in early 2018 that detail how the authority is regulating ICOs and cryptocurrencies depending on their function and transferability. FINMA categorizes tokens in three types, payment tokens, utility tokens and asset tokens, but hybrid forms exist too.

Thailand

Thailand allows ICOs and cryptocurrency trading. The Securities and Exchange Commission has released a statement paper, welcoming the use of Altcoins, but leaving open the possibility of regulating Altcoins thought to be securities.

Conclusion

At this point, you should understand what Blockchain technology and cryptocurrency is, and you should be equipped with the knowledge of what to look out for when evaluating investments be it ICOs or trading cryptocurrencies on an exchange, as well as the landscape of cryptocurrencies. You should also have an idea of the opportunities and the risks available in this exciting era but you must always keep in mind that the landscape is constantly changing and with it strategies for investing will evolve alongside.

While many people end up losing money, there are always those that profit from trading and investing. Moreover, cryptocurrencies have given the opportunity to change economic classes if you do it well.

Investing and trading is a skill, and like any other skill you cannot expect to be a master overnight. It takes a lot of practice and learning, so start small and do not jump in with both feet. The key is to keep up to date with the strategies and closely follow the developments in the industry, after all as Warren Buffet advises, "never invest in a business you cannot understand".

I wish you all the best in your journey, and thank you for taking the time to read this book!

If you enjoyed this book, please take the time to leave me a review on Amazon. I appreciate your honest feedback, and it really helps me to continue producing high quality books.

www.ingramcontent.com/pod-product-compliance
Lightning Source LLC
Chambersburg PA
CBHW070122230526
45472CB00004B/1384